10/10

W9-BDK-975

Grasshoppers

ABDO
Publishing Company

Big Buddy BOOKS
Insects

Julie Murray

Published by ABDO Publishing Company, 8000 West 78th Street, Edina, Minnesota 55439.

Printed in the United States of America, North Mankato, Minnesota.
042010
092010

 PRINTED ON RECYCLED PAPER

Coordinating Series Editor: Rochelle Baltzer
Editor: Sarah Tieck
Contributing Editors: Heidi M.D. Elston, Megan M. Gunderson, BreAnn Rumsch, Marcia Zappa
Graphic Design: Maria Hosley
Cover Photograph: *Image Ideas Inc.*
Interior Photographs/Illustrations: *AnimalsAnimals-Earth Scenes*: ©BEATTY, BILL (p. 23), ©WECHSLER, DOUG (p. 15); *iStockphoto*: ©iStockphoto.com/LindaCharlton (p. 30), ©iStockphoto.com/prill (p. 29); *Peter Arnold, Inc.*: ©Biosphoto/Borrell Bartomeu (p. 17), ©Biosphoto/Michel & Christine Denis-Huot (p. 21), ©Biosphoto/Nicaise Thierry (pp. 23, 30), Matt Meadows (p. 13); *Photo Researchers, Inc.*: E.R. Degginger (p. 9), Stephen J. Krasemann (p. 19), Francesco Tomasinelli (p. 26), Paul Whitten (p. 27); *Shutterstock*: ahnhuynh (p. 25), alle (p. 5), ansem (p. 5), André Gonçalves (p. 11), Leighton Photography & Imaging (p. 5), livestock99 (p. 7), Brett Stoltz (p. 5), Martin Valigursky (p. 5).

Library of Congress Cataloging-in-Publication Data

Murray, Julie, 1969-
 Grasshoppers / Julie Murray.
   p. cm. -- (Insects)
 ISBN 978-1-61613-486-0
 1. Grasshoppers--Juvenile literature. I. Title. II. Series: Murray, Julie, 1969- Insects.
 QL508.A2M953 2011
 595.7'26--dc22
                        2010002525

Contents

Insect World

Millions of insects live throughout the world. They are found on the ground, in the air, and in the water. Insects have existed since before there were dinosaurs!

Grasshoppers are one type of insect. They live around the world in grassy, leafy areas. If you look closely, you might find grasshoppers in your backyard!

Bug Bite!

Grasshoppers are closely related to crickets and katydids.

Grasshoppers come in many different colors.

A Grasshopper's Body

Like all insects, grasshoppers have three main body parts. These are the head, the **thorax**, and the **abdomen**.

A grasshopper's head has a mouth with strong **jaws**. It also has two very large eyes, three smaller eyes, and two antennae. Antennae help grasshoppers touch and smell things.

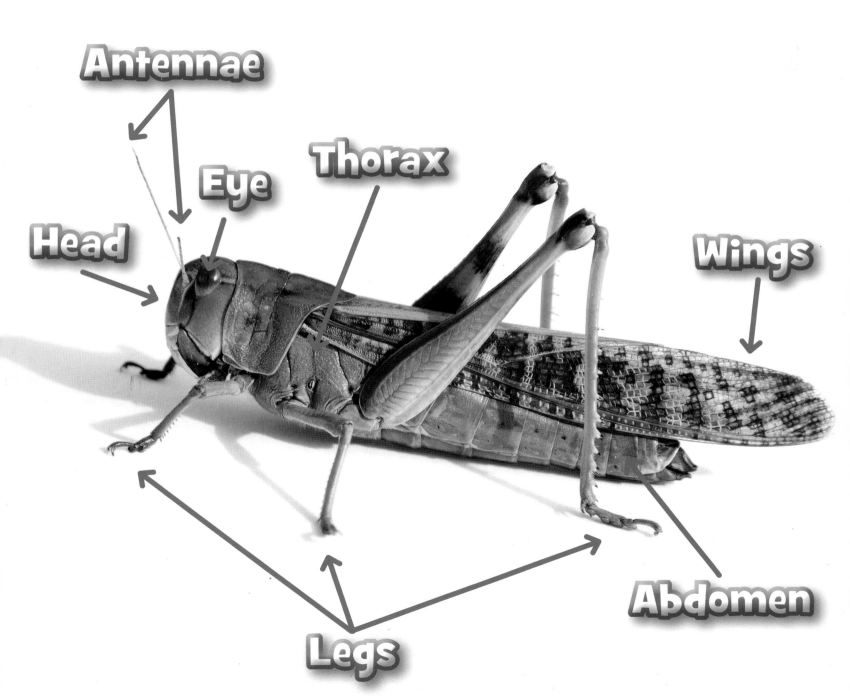

Antennae

Eye

Thorax

Head

Wings

Legs

Abdomen

Six legs connect to the **thorax**. Most grasshoppers also have two pairs of wings on the thorax. Important **organs** are inside a grasshopper's **abdomen**.

Bug Bite!

There are more than 10,000 different types of grasshoppers.

Only adult grasshoppers with wings can fly. They often do this when they are frightened or bothered.

Strong Legs

Grasshopper bodies are made to move. All three pairs of legs help a grasshopper walk. But, its back legs are special.

A grasshopper has **muscular** back legs. This helps it push off the ground to make big leaps! These two legs are often a different color from the other four.

Many grasshoppers have feet hooks. These help them grab hold of plants they land on.

Life Begins

The grasshopper life cycle has three stages. These are egg, nymph (NIHMF), and adult.

Like other insects, grasshoppers begin life as eggs. Male and female grasshoppers usually **mate** in late summer or fall. Then, the female lays her eggs in a safe place.

Life Cycle of an Eastern Lubber Grasshopper

Egg

Nymph

Adult

Inside the eggs, nymphs begin growing. Most mother and father grasshoppers die as winter approaches. Grasshopper nymphs usually **hatch** in spring. Then, they must care for themselves.

Nymphs look like adult grasshoppers. But, they are much smaller and do not yet have wings.

Bug Bite!

Female grasshoppers lay eggs using their ovipositor. The ovipositor is on the end of the abdomen.

Grasshoppers lay eggs in hidden areas, such as holes in logs or underground.

Growing Up

Nymphs eat plants. As they eat, their bodies grow bigger. They become too big for their skin, so they **shed**. This uncovers new skin underneath. This process is called molting.

Bug Bite!

When a grasshopper nymph molts, its skin splits along its back. Then, it crawls out.

Like adult grasshoppers, nymphs are herbivores. They eat grass, crops, and many other plants.

A Grasshopper's Life

A nymph **sheds** about five times. After the last time, it is an adult. Adult grasshoppers are fully grown. Many have two pairs of wings and can fly. Adults can also **mate**. Most adult grasshoppers live just a few months.

A grasshopper's wings usually lay flat on its back. They provide layers of protection for the body. But when grasshoppers fly, they fan out their wings.

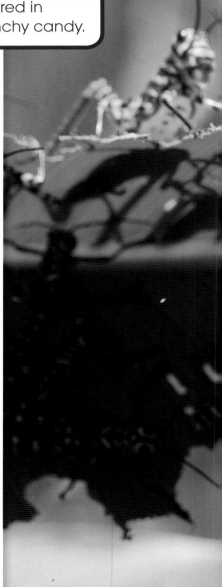

Some people eat grasshoppers covered in chocolate. They say this snack is like a crunchy candy.

Adult grasshoppers spend their short lives in grassy or leafy areas. They are most active during the day.

Adult grasshoppers are hungry! They like to eat leaves, flowers, and grasses. Their strong **jaws** help them bite and chew plants.

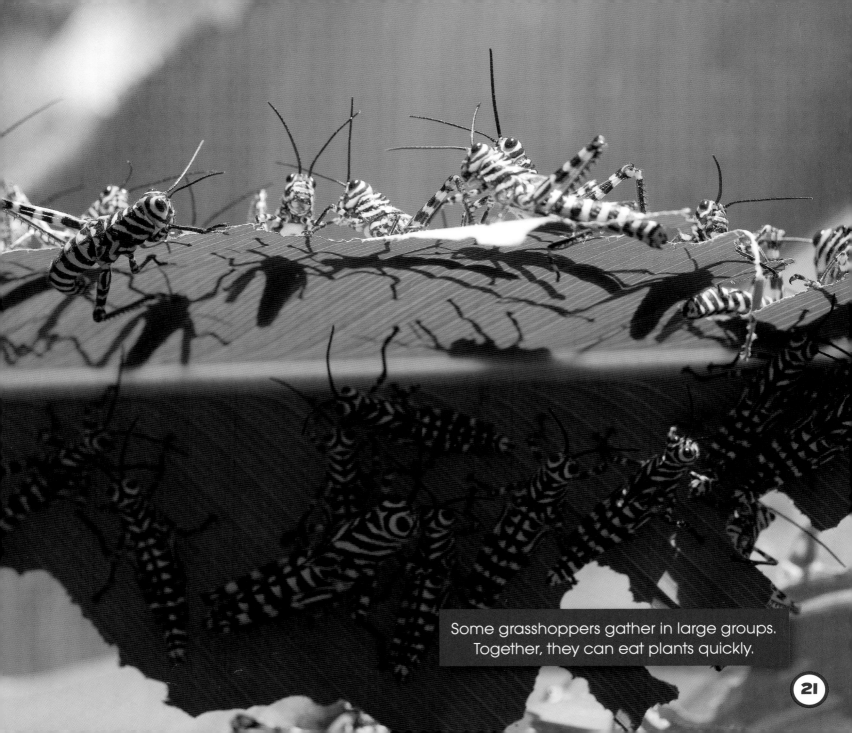

Some grasshoppers gather in large groups.
Together, they can eat plants quickly.

Musical Bugs

Grasshoppers use their bodies to make sounds, or "sing." This is one way they talk to each other. Most grasshoppers who sing are male.

To sing, a grasshopper rubs its back leg over its wing. It makes different sounds by changing the speed of the movements.

Grasshoppers make sounds in a way similar to how a person plays a violin. A grasshopper's legs and wings move like a violin's bow and strings.

Toothlike ridges on a grasshopper's back leg help the grasshopper sing.

Good Listeners

Grasshoppers don't have ears like humans do. Instead, they have hearing **organs**. Usually, these organs are hidden near the base of the **abdomen**. Grasshoppers listen to each other's songs with these organs.

Bug Bite!

Different types of grass make different sou

Grasshopper hearing organs are called tympanal organs.

Some grasshoppers make a poisonous yellow foam. It can be powerful enough to keep away large predators, such as tarantulas!

Danger Zone

Grasshoppers face many predators. Birds, spiders, and other animals eat them.

Can you see the grasshopper hiding in the leaves?

Grasshoppers have different ways to **protect** themselves. They can jump or fly away. The coloring of some grasshoppers matches their surroundings. Others let out a smelly liquid if a predator is near.

Special Insects

Grasshoppers are an important part of the food chain. They serve as food for many animals. And, they eat certain plants. This helps keep the natural world in balance.

Some farmers and gardeners consider grasshoppers pests. Grasshoppers can destroy whole fields of plants!

Bug Bite!

Scientists who study insects are called entomologists (ehn-tuh-MAH-luh-jihsts).

Bug-O-Rama

How big are grasshoppers?

One South American grasshopper can reach more than four inches (10 cm) long! That's about the length of a computer mouse.

What is one talented grasshopper?

Band-winged grasshoppers can make crackling sounds while flying.

Do grasshoppers have superpowers?

Well, not really. But, the Eastern lubber grasshopper makes a smelly brown liquid. This may keep away insect predators, such as ants.

Are grasshoppers picky eaters?

No! Grasshoppers eat just about any kind of plant. And, some have eaten screen doors and clothing!

Important Words

abdomen (AB-duh-muhn) the back part of an insect's body.

hatch to be born from an egg.

jaws a mouthpart that allows for holding, crushing, and chewing.

mate to join as a couple in order to reproduce, or have babies.

muscular (MUHS-kyuh-luhr) having strong, well-developed muscles. Muscles are body tissues, or layers of cells, that help the body move.

organ a body part that does a special job. The heart and the lungs are organs.

protect (pruh-TEHKT) to guard against harm or danger.

shed to cast aside or lose as part of a natural process of life.

thorax the middle part of an insect's body.

Web Sites

To learn more about grasshoppers, visit ABDO Publishing Company online. Web sites about grasshoppers are featured on our Book Links page. These links are routinely monitored and updated to provide the most current information available.

www.abdopublishing.com

Index